MODIGLIANI
THE
SCULPTOR

Alfred Werner

MODIGLIANI

THE

SCULPTOR

A Golden Griffin Book / Arts, Inc., New York

Frontispiece: *Amedeo Modigliani standing beside one of his stone heads. From copy of old photograph; courtesy of M. Maurice Lefebvre-Foinet, Paris.*

Library of Congress Catalogue Card Number 61-18347.
© 1962, Arts, Inc., 667 Madison Avenue, New York, N. Y.

84924

To Judith

Table of Contents

"Sculpture was his main passion, his real vocation", says Bernard Dorival, art historian and Director of the Musée National d'Art Moderne in Paris about Amedeo Modigliani. The persons closest to the artist in his life were aware that his supreme yearning was to realize himself not as a painter but as a sculptor. Yet he has been generally known to the public as a painter.

This is the first book on Modigliani's sculpture that has ever been published and it is the hope of the publishers that this deeply significant part of Modigliani's work will now become better known to lovers of art. The surviving works of sculpture are very few. With the exception of those which could not be traced or for which permission to reproduce was not granted, they are all represented here by one or more photographs.

The twenty-six caryatids included in the book are reproductions of drawings—in gouache, pencil, water color, and mixed media—intended by Modigliani as preparation for a great series of sculptured caryatids that he dreamed of producing. They form an important part of his sculptural vision, even though, except for the stone caryatid now in the Museum of Modern Art, he never managed to translate them into actual sculpture. Thus, we hope that this large selection of variations upon a single basic image may help to promote insight into the workings of Modigliani's imagination as a sculptor and into the values he was trying to achieve.

Dr. Werner's essay conveys the vitality of Modigliani's art. He treats Modigliani's career, setting the sculptural output in the framework of Modigliani's whole effort. He provides a richly circumstantial account of the relationship between Modigliani the sculptor and Modigliani the painter. When one has read this essay, one can understand the paradox of Modigliani the

sculptor. For there is a paradox. Most of Modigliani's sculpture was produced within a period of five years prior to the outbreak of the First World War. Afterwards, he abandoned sculpture for painting, in the end even ceasing to think of himself as a sculptor.

If this book helps to restore unity to a vision disrupted by the circumstances of Modigliani's life, it will be worth the effort to all who have contributed to it.

The publishers wish to express their gratitude to the many persons and institutions who permitted them to reproduce these works. They are under special obligation to those who provided photographs, among them are included: Mr. Edgardo Acosta, the Edgardo Acosta Gallery, Beverly Hills; Mr. and Mrs. James W. Alsdorf, Winnetka, Illinois; Mr. and Mrs. John Cowles, Minneapolis, Minnesota; Mr. Jean Masurel, Roubaix, France; Mr. and Mrs. Chester Dale, New York City; Mr. and Mrs. Deltcheff, Paris; Mrs. Nelson Gutman, Baltimore, Maryland; Mr. and Mrs. Morton D. May, St. Louis, Missouri; Mr. and Mrs. Joseph Pulitzer, Jr., St. Louis, Missouri; Mr. and Mrs. Gustave Ring, Washington, D. C.; the Baltimore Museum of Art, Baltimore, Maryland; the Barnes Foundation, Merion, Pennsylvania; the Solomon R. Guggenheim Museum, New York City; the Hanover Gallery, London; the Marion Koogler McNay Art Institute, San Antonio, Texas; the Musée National d'Art Moderne, Paris; the Museum of Modern Art, New York City; the Norton Gallery and School of Art, West Palm Beach, Florida; the Philadelphia Museum of Art, Philadelphia, Pennsylvania; the Seattle Art Museum, Seattle, Washington; and the Tate Gallery, London.

The editors could never have collected these reproductions without advice and assistance from many quarters. It was necessary in the first place to locate the originals, and although the whereabouts of some of the works were easily discovered, others had to be patiently traced, sometimes through several changes of ownership, sometimes with only the scantiest initial clues. We are grateful to all who helped in this work. We wish to express special thanks to the following persons who furnished various kinds of indispensable aid and information: Mr. K. J. Hewett, London; the staff of the Parke-Bernet Galleries; Mr. Henry Pearlman, the Henry Pearlman Foundation, New York City; Mr. Herbert Singer, New York City; Miss Erica Brausen, the Hanover Gallery, London; Miss Adelyn D. Breeskin, the Baltimore Museum of Art; Mrs. Donna Butler and Miss Sally McLean, the Solomon R. Guggenheim Museum; Mr. Perry B. Cott, the National Gallery of Art, Washington, D.C.; Mr. Bernard Dorival, the Musée National d'Art Moderne, Paris; Mr. Henry G. Gardiner, the Philadelphia Museum of Art; Mr. Francisco Matarazzo Sobrinho, the Museu de Arte Moderna, São Paulo, Brazil; Miss Pearl Moeller, the Museum of Modern Art; Miss Agnes Mongan, Fogg Art Museum, Harvard University; Miss Gertrude Rosenthal, the Baltimore Museum of Art; Mr. Peter Selz and Mr. Willard Tangen, the Museum of Modern Art; Miss Emily Hartwell Tupper, the Seattle Art Museum; Miss Katherine Waldram, Tate Gallery, London.

Special gratitude is due to Madame Jeanne Modigliani Nechtschein, daughter of the sculptor, for her counsel; to Dr. Marco Valsecchi of Milan, Italy, and to Mr. Klaus G. Perls of Perls Galleries, New York City, for their expert advice concerning various works by Modigliani; to Mr. Sam Cauman for his manifold editorial assistance; to Mr. Otto Fried, who furnished advice on the layout of the book; to Mrs. Valia Hirsch who read the text; and to Miss Zita Vlavianos, who conducted the detailed work of collecting the photographs and contributed largely to the planning and editing of the book.

Thanks are due as well to Mr. Victor Weiss and Mrs. Doris Schiff for their faithful cooperation in the production of the book.

Modigliani the Sculptor

IN ITALY, AN ODD LEGAL PROVISION relating to the seizure of a debtor's property forbids the officers of the law to impound a bed in which a woman has just given birth to a child. Only this provision made possible a modicum of comfort for Eugenia, wife of the bankrupt businessman Flaminio Modigliani when, on July 12, 1884, she gave birth to their fourth child, Amedeo ("beloved of God"). The Modigliani family had moved into a shabby apartment only a few days earlier, having been forced by poverty to leave the house in a more elegant section of Leghorn (Livorno) in which they had lived for over a decade. Mother and child were covered by a mound of family possessions, piled on the bed so as to be saved from confiscation. Roaming about the dreary empty rooms were three other children: Emmanuele, born in 1872; Margherita, born in 1874; and Umberto, born in 1878—all of them old enough to sense tragedy and comprehend their parents' grief.

Thus did one of the most remarkable artists of our century enter the world. The popular notion still has it that Amedeo Modigliani came of a wealthy family, and, as spurious anecdotes and absurd legends about his life in Paris were put into circulation after his death by persons who claimed to have known him, further misinformation encrusted his image.

His family was Sephardic, one of the old Jewish families of Italy, where, as in most Latin countries, Jews generally mixed with the gentiles around them and took on the appearance and behavior of their neighbors to a much greater degree than did their brethren in the North and the East. In Paris, Modigliani was usually considered a typical Italian, whereas Chagall and Soutine were regarded not as Russian and Lithu-

anian, but as Jews. All who met Modigliani were struck by his aristocratic bearing even at the depth of misery and self-neglect, and this contributed further to the myth of family wealth.

Although he was brought up in the Jewish faith, later in life he became an agnostic (and a socialist). His deepest faith, however, was art, which he had already embraced in early adolescence.

At the age of fourteen, sick with typhoid fever during a vacation from school, he raved in his delirium about the paintings in the Palazzo Pitti and the Uffizi in Florence, where he had never been, and wept because he could not go to see them. This was the first clear sign of his future vocation. His mother, deeply worried, assured him that as soon as he recovered they would go to Florence together. She kept her promise. Shortly after the trip, with tuition money provided by a relative, she also sent him to the best art teacher in Leghorn, a painter named Guglielmo Micheli. Amedeo worked with him from 1898 to 1900.

Micheli, who was born in 1866 and died in 1926, lived long enough to hear of his pupil's posthumous fame. He seems to have been a competent teacher, giving the boy much more in the way of technical training than the latter was ever to acknowledge. Though himself a mediocre artist, Micheli was probably one of the best masters Italy had to offer at a time when Italian art generally lacked creative personalities. He belonged to the most progressive Italian school of the period, a group known as the "Macchiaioli" (from *macchia*—"dash of color"), whose members, like the French Impressionists, had discovered the open air, farm cottages, country roads, and the radiance of the sun on earth and water. But the freshness of their subject matter was not matched by a real freshness of technique, and the stale air of the academy clung to their work.

Modigliani's apprenticeship was relatively brief, and the known details are few. In 1900 he was forced to break off his studies because he had contracted tuberculosis. He was treated at the local clinic, but no effective cure for the disease had been developed, and the infection was not completely eliminated. (Two decades later when he was in his mid-thirties, dissipation, fatigue, and malnutrition brought on a fatal return of his illness.) For the time being, however, the sunshine south of Tuscany, where Signora Modigliani sent her son, did arrest the illness. The eager student used the rest cure as an opportunity to travel and visit the art galleries and to see the old as well as the new Italian masters.

On his return from the south, Amedeo was urged by his mother to take the examinations for the Florence Academy of Art. He passed, but does not seem to have done much studying at the academy, though he lived and worked in Florence all through 1902 and 1903. The better part of the next three years were probably spent in Venice. Periodically he returned to his native Leghorn to see his family—more precisely, his beloved mother. A photograph taken in 1904, when he was twenty, shows him as an unusually handsome, healthy-looking young man, with thick dark hair, thoughtful eyes, and a soft dreamy mouth.

In Venice he associated with a Spanish artist, Ortiz de Zarate, who describes him as a dandy popular with the ladies. De Zarate says also that Modigliani was still painting in an academic manner at that time. According to Umberto Brunelleschi, another artist, who knew him there, he gave no signs of exceptional talent.

Unfortunately, little of the work Modigliani did before going to Paris seems to have survived. But written and unchallengeable evidence exists that even before Paris he had adopted a nonacademic, anticonventional outlook on life and art. It is this which makes us question the validity of the critic Florent Fels' assertion, that had Modigliani not left Italy he would never have become an important modernist. ("Had he remained in . . . his beloved Italy . . . he would have satisfied his romantic taste—that very taste which, in Paris, he violently expunged from his soul with great strength.") Paris produced neither his talent nor his neurosis. It did, however, enhance the morbid symptoms of both. It is possible that had Modigliani never left Italy he might have lived more soberly, and longer, though there probably would have been the same artistic rebellion.

There is evidence for such a probability in five lengthy letters written from the south, in 1901, by the seventeen-year-old traveler to his close friend Oscar Ghiglia (1879-1945). Ghiglia and Modigliani had first met in Micheli's studio, and the friendship had grown during prolonged discussions as together they walked the beaches of Leghorn. In 1902, the year after these letters were written, they shared a room in Florence, and the next year they both had studios there. But after 1903 their ardent friendship seems to have ended, for reasons unknown to us.

Ghiglia, who was several years older than Modigliani, was not an outstanding artist, but was a responsive sounding-board for Amedeo's enthusiasm. In these letters—all that survive of an extensive correspondence—the adolescent Modigliani emerges as an admirer of Baudelaire and Nietzsche, but unfortunately he makes all too few references to painting. It is significant that he refers disdainfully to his old teacher Micheli, whom he begins to consider highly unoriginal: "Micheli?" he writes from Capri. "Oh my God, how many of his kind there are in Capri . . . regiments!"

Nietzschean is Modigliani's idea that life should be fully lived, without concern for obstacles, but with definite, purposeful intent, and sometimes even in pain, in order to "save one's own dream." And he urges his friend to cultivate as sacred all "that can exalt and excite your intelligence," and to "seek to provoke . . . and create . . . these fertile stimuli, because they can push the intelligence to its maximum creative power."

According to these letters, art for the young Modigliani was not a trade to be learned by diligent application, but rather a state of grace achieved by intellectual elevation. When this exalted state is attained, the state that follows "the awakening and dissolution of powerful energies," the state in which "excitement" (*orgasmo*) is induced, then, and only then, does one know the joy of creation, which is at the same time a liberation. ". . . I am rich and fertile now, and I need work," Modigliani cries.

Whatever de Zarate and Brunelleschi may have thought of Amedeo's early work, this certainly is not the language of a conventional student. From Capri the young artist writes that he is waiting for the right moment "for organizing myself . . . and for working . . . in the good sense of the word, that is to say, to dedicate myself with faith (body and soul) to *organizing* and *developing* all the impressions, all the germs of ideas, that I have harvested in this peace, as in a mystic garden." On his visit to the Eternal City the seventeen-year-old enthusiast extols "the Rome that while I speak to you, is not outside, but *inside* me, like a terrible jewel fastened upon its seven hills, like seven imperious ideas . . . Rome is the orchestration with which I encircle myself, the circumscribed area within which I isolate myself and in which I concentrate my thought. Its feverish sweetness, its tragic countryside, its beautiful and harmonious forms, all these things are mine through my thought and through my work . . . I seek further to formulate with the greatest possible lucidity the truths about art and life that I have gleaned meagerly from among the beauties of Rome . . ."

In another letter Amedeo talks to Oscar about his emotional stresses and difficulties: "They are all necessary stages of evolution through which we have to pass and which have no importance other than the end to which they lead. Believe me, the work that has arrived by now at its final stage of gestation, and which has become depersonalized by the obstacle of all particular incidents that have contributed to its fertilization and production, is not worth the trouble of being expressed and translated in style. The efficacy and necessity of style consists exactly in this: that beyond being the only vocabulary capable of bringing out an idea, it detaches it [the idea] from the individual who has produced it [and] leaves the way open to that which cannot or should not be uttered . . ."

In the last of these early letters—what a pity that so very little of Modigliani's correspondence has been preserved!—he again refers to his own and his friend's growing pains: "Affirm and surpass always. The man who does not know how to continually release new desires from his energy, to release an almost new individual destined always to express himself by laying low all that is old and rotten, is not a man, he is a bourgeois, a real knave, or what you will . . ."

It is possible, even likely, that a few years later the artist would have smiled at these manifestations of juvenile exuberance. But I doubt that he would have repudiated them, for his idealism remained with him throughout his short and agitated life. To the very end he would have endorsed what he wrote when only seventeen: "Beauty . . . has some painful duties; these duties create, nevertheless, the most beautiful expressions of the soul."

In any event, it was predictable that the youth who penned these letters would soon find a place like Leghorn too narrow and confining. In Venice, he heard from his friend de Zarate a great deal about Montmartre and its artists' colony, and by 1906 he was ready to go there. Financed by his family and fortified by his mother's good wishes, he took the train for France.

As soon as he had arrived in Paris, it became obvious that a mere geographical move was not enough—an inner break with his past was necessary. Ironically, the young man who had been so bold and unconventional in his letters was now shocked and even repelled by the atmsophere of the French capital. It was precisely in Montmartre that he felt most uncomfortable, discovering that he was, after all, a provincial instead of a free-living Bohemian.

It did not help much that he changed his style of dress to corduroys, scarlet scarf, and a big black hat; he still looked like a bourgeois at a masquerade. Nor did he become any the more a Bohemian by renting a studio on the Rue Caulaincourt, in the center of the artists' quarter, and furnishing it with a piano, plush drapes, a plaster cast of Beethoven's head, and reproductions of Italian Renaissance paintings. For a while he remained the dutiful, sober student away from home, writing regularly to his mother, and weeping with homesickness when he read her letters. He punctually attended the famous Colarossi school on the Rue Chaumière and diligently sketched from the nude, but always cupping his hand over his work to hide the results from fellow students. He drank mild Italian wine—and nothing else—in moderation, had no vices, and kept his bachelor apartment neat. Being unsure of himself, this timid, almost reserved Italian would not discuss art with strangers. He was astonishingly conservative in his views. Once, when Picasso passed him in a café, Modigliani made a derogatory remark about his wearing the dirty clothes of workmen: Picasso might have talent, he said, but that did not excuse his uncouth appearance.

The break with the past finally came before Modigliani had spent a full year in Paris. One day a visiting friend found his atelier completely changed. It was in a state of chaos; the Renaissance reproductions had been stuffed away into a box; and as for the studio's occupant himself—he was now an alcoholic and a drug addict. But far more important, he had also become a revolutionary in the realm of art. We do not know precisely what caused this transformation from a bourgeois into a *"peintre maudit,"* nor are we sure of the exact moment—if there was one—at which it took place. But we do know that the critic and poet André Salmon later insisted that Modigliani's talent was due to his vices: "From the day he abandoned himself to certain forms of debauchery an unexpected light came upon him, transforming his art. From that day on he became one who must be counted among the masters of living art." Another biographer, Charles Douglas, quoting the painter André Utter—husband of Suzanne Valadon and stepfather of Utrillo—describes the circumstances under which Modigliani's metamorphosis as an artist, if not as a man, took place: "One night, at an alcohol and hashish orgy *chez* Pigard . . . Modigliani suddenly gave a yell and, grabbing paper and pencil, began to draw feverishly, shouting that he had found 'the way.' When he had finished, he triumphantly produced a study of a woman's head and the swan neck for which he has become famous."

There is, of course, no medical justification for suggesting that either alcohol or hashish made Modigliani "invent" the characteristic features of his mature style. They merely helped the timid and inhibited newcomer to proceed faster toward that release of which he had dreamed in his juvenile letters. Because he wanted to be free to "distort"—that is, to force his own artistic vision upon reality—he decided, apparently, that he had to live the life that would, as he saw it, assure him the maximum of freedom. Alcohol, hashish, and sexual promiscuity were a means of liberating himself from Leghorn and all it stood for. And he knew that his family, even his beloved mother, would reject as crazy his new way of painting.

The Jews of Leghorn lived sober lives, drank nothing stronger than wine, married early, and raised families. But this rebel chose for a drinking companion the painter Utrillo, an alcoholic who would not have been admitted to Flaminio Modigliani's apartment. Modigliani also had affairs with women of all sorts, all most unlike his mother—models, waitresses, prostitutes. His whole life became a succession of protests: against the the bourgeois smugness of his family of impoverished bankers, against his old art teacher Micheli, and against a society that refused to recognize and reward his talent.

Picasso once remarked on his exhibitionism: "You can find Utrillo drunk anywhere . . . but Modigliani is always drunk right in front of the Rotonde or the Dôme"—that is, where he could be seen by writers, critics, and fellow artists. Often he was carried to extremes: when he got drunk enough at social gatherings, he would strip to the skin. This exhibitionism was but one aspect of the desire for self-expression that led him always to put something of his own nature into his subjects. What some of his contemporaries took for exaggerated self-assertion was an intense longing to find an identity to stamp on the world. In his *roman à clef, Les Montparnos,* Michel Georges—Michel draws a good picture of Modigliani when he has the hero, Madrulleau, exclaim: "I need a flame in order to paint, in order to be consumed by fire. My concierge and the butcher boy have no need of alcohol, especially if it does them harm. They must conserve their precious lives . . . But as for me, my life, it is important only because of what I put on my canvas . . . So what difference does it make if I give an instant of my life, if in exchange I can create a work that, perhaps, will last."

With this statement, we lose all trace of "Dedo," the dreamy, pampered youth from Leghorn, and enter a phase that might be termed "Modigliani the Damned."

The rest of the story is so well known that it need not be repeated here in detail. Modigliani had a dozen reckless years of life left, and except for two short trips to Italy, where his family tried in vain to reform him, he spent them all in Paris ruining himself systematically. He smoked incessantly. Under the influence of alcohol and drugs he made long, shocking speeches before the astonished patrons of bistros. When arrested after a riotous scene, he also startled the police with impassioned and dramatic recitals of poetry.

He had a hypnotic fascination for women. He could give them little, not even his undivided attention, but this did not keep them from throwing themselves at him, and they were only too eager to supply him with everything he needed: brushes, colors, canvases, alcohol, drugs and, naturally, sex. Flitting from woman to woman, he never married, but eventually he found a girl, Jeanne Hébuterne, sufficiently self-effacing to be able to live with him in a stable relationship. When a daughter was born to them, "Modi" made an effort to register himself as father, but on the way to the municipal office he stopped at a bar and forgot his errand. Time and again the beautiful Jeanne would follow him to his favorite café, to cajole him to come back home with her before he became too drunk to walk. And she followed him in death. On January 25, 1920 her beloved died in a charity hospital of tubercular meningitis.[1] The next day, Jeanne Hébuterne flung herself from a fifth-story window.

The most touching obituary was written by the poet, Francis Carco:

"A life marked by poverty, worry, the desire to escape platitudes by contradictions, by the wish to surpass, by thirst for punishment and the willingness to become a target for the supposedly astute. Life of an artist, life of exaltations! I shall not recount the picturesque bohemianisms of it, or the paradoxical and constant defiance of rule, or the absence of all traces of domesticity. But for all that, for all the defects and qualities, the taste for unhappiness and the exceptional, the torrent of graces, the deliriousness and the naughtiness, Modigliani leaves a void behind him that cannot soon be filled."

Modigliani captivated countless people by the wit and charm he could display even when totally drunk. One of them was the Polish-born poet and art dealer, Leopold Zborowski. At a time when nearly everybody else thought Modigliani a madman and without talent, Zborowski was firmly convinced of his genius, and he badgered every art patron he knew to come and see his friend's work. But very few canvases were sold, and even those at ridiculously low prices; Modigliani remained wretchedly poor to the end of his days.

Zborowski survived his protégé by twelve years —he died in 1932—and lived to see Modigliani's name celebrated. In 1922, only two years after the artist's death, the museum in Grenoble bought one of his pictures, the first in a long succession to be acquired by museums; in the same year a retrospective exhibition of his work was held at the Galerie Bernheim-Jeune in Paris. Eight years later the celebrated Venice· Biennale included about fifty of Modigliani's works in an effort to make amends to an artist who during his lifetime had been so sorely neglected.

There are certain features by which even a layman can recognize Modigliani's elegant portraits of Montmartre and Montparnasse characters, as well as his lush yet somehow virginal nudes. But it is not for its mannerisms that his art has become immortal, nor is it these that lead people to pay over one hundred thousand dollars for one of his canvases. The important thing is that Modigliani created formal and universal beauty in perpetuating the essentials of a face or a body.

Living as he did, it is surprising that he produced drawings, paintings and sculpture composed with a cool purposefulness, firm in line, color, and over-all design. If art were a simple reflection of biography, one would expect of Modigliani torrents of orgiastic color, untidily smeared on the canvas in thick impasto, as found in the work of his *copain* Soutine. But if he did not have the strength to fight his alcoholism, in the sober intervals he did dedicate himself to the most complete and perfect aesthetic transfiguration of his inner imagery that he was capable of. This was amply demonstrated in each of the more than twenty memorial shows.

Not enough stress, however, is paid to the purely spiritual aspects of his art in the numerous biographies, the first of which was by his friend André Salmon. Most of the tales dwell on the "beatnik" aspects of his life rather than on the occasions when his intrinsic *noblesse* and genuine humility came to the fore. There are two significant stories. One is in the excellent book by the Swiss critic Gotthard Jedlicka, which still remains to be translated into English. Modigliani, we are told, had a boundless admiration for Cézanne (though they had very different temperaments, and though only such early works of Modigliani as the *Cellist* and the *Beggar of Leghorn* are Cézannesque, mainly in their distortions). Whenever Cézanne's name was mentioned, a reverent expression would come over Modigliani's face. He would, with a slow and secretive gesture, take from his pocket a reproduction of *Boy with Red Vest*, hold it up to his face like a breviary, and draw it to his lips and kiss it. Another illuminating detail is given by Franco Russoli. Summoned to paint the portrait of a collector, Modigliani, upon spotting a work by Picasso in the apartment, exclaimed: "How great he is; he's always ten years ahead of the rest of us."[2] He begged the owner to leave it beside him while he painted, so that it would serve as an example and inspiration.

This deification of art by the painter seems to be far more significant than any of the acts of exhibitionism which he may have committed around the bars of Montmartre and Montparnasse. Modigliani is one of the finest representatives of the school which holds that art grows upon art, not upon the observation of nature alone. His work is the very antithesis of Courbet's or Pissarro's, and it seems linked in spirit to Delacroix, who repeatedly warned against too close imitation of nature, or to Degas, who quipped that a picture requires as much knavery, trickery, and deceit as the perpetration of a crime.

For Modigliani, nature played no important role. He never painted a still life, and produced only two landscapes—if one may apply this term to the hard, dry renderings of Midi vistas he made toward the end of his career. Unlike Pissarro, he never portrayed people amid green foliage. The background is nearly always simple color—aquamarine, turquoise, green, gray or brown. His portraits and his studies of nudes use people only as points of departure. His works are pictures rather than slices of life. Whistler called his mother's portrait *Arrangement in Gray and Black* ("It must stand or fall on its merits as an 'arrangement' "). Modigliani, who initially admired Whistler, might very well have described his own pictures as "Arrangements of Ovoids and Cylinders," had he been given to pedantic language.

Undoubtedly Modigliani was a forerunner of abstract art only in a remote sense—even less than was his mentor Brancusi (who, it should be emphasized, also remained to the very end attached to perceptual subject matter). Still, he can be classified with the purists in art (all "abstract" to a degree), from the medieval Primitives of his native Tuscany to the Pre-Raphaelite Brotherhood, to the Pointillists, to the maverick Whistler who willy-nilly contributed to the anti-naturalistic trend that has reached its apogee in our time.

But Modigliani as a purist, or an abstractionist, was *sui generis*. While, for instance, Whistler's predominantly decorative portrait studies may leave one cold, those of Modigliani are filled with fire; they are aflame, but not consumed. Whenever Modigliani is called an Expressionist there is a clamor of protest from those to whom Expressionism means exclusively the impasto of a Van Gogh, the morbidly sensitive line of a Schiele, the loaded brush of a Soutine, the furious attack on canvas by the early Kokoschka, or the brutal chromatics of a Nolde. Modigliani, master of equilibrium, somehow succeeded in imposing a sterner aesthetic unity upon formal and psychological elements than any of these artists, and such classical finesse might seem to exclude him from their company. But Expressionism's stress is on *inwardness* rather than on anything else, while the distortions or exaggerations of the ordinary forms and colors of nature are not ends in themselves.

The Milan scholar Paolo D'Ancona defined Expressionism as "an effort, *no matter how carried out* [italics mine], to focus on man, or rather on the inner side of man," which derives "from impulse and spontaneous human sympathy"—a broad definition that allowed D'Ancona to put

Modigliani and Pascin side by side with Soutine and Chagall. Those who narrowly trace Expressionism to *Die Bruecke* and nothing else should be reminded of Benedetto Croce's *Estetica* (published in 1902), with its emphasis on "intuition," which, sparking Expressionism, preceded the Dresden group by several years.

Modigliani is as much a true Expressionist as is, for instance, Soutine, and one critic has even insisted that "underneath the broken and distorted surfaces, the swirling Prussian blues and brick-reds, the form of Soutine's figures is very nearly identical with Modigliani's skittle-shaped ladies and gentlemen." Modigliani's work is classically firm but not cold; wise but not overintellectual. If this patrician Leghorn Jew, blown by a strange wind from the quasi-Impressionist studio of his first teacher, Guglielmo Micheli, and from the conservative ottocento academies of Florence and Venice into the seething caldron of Paris, can be associated with any school at all, it would be with that of Expressionism. For though there is Fauve color in some of his early painting, the anti-classical "beastliness" of the Fauves was not for him, and though there is a faint echo of cubism in the stereometric forms to which his figures can be reduced, the Cubists were too rational, too calculating, for his fervent soul. Futurism, with its proto-Fascist glorification of the machine and war, its hatred of the nude and the art of the museums, was anathema to him—so much so that he refused to sign the Futurist Manifesto, even though all the originators of the movement were Italians like himself.

It is puzzling how Modigliani succeeded where others failed: how he could be both representational and nonrepresentational at the same time, could fulfill the demands of the much more rigid purists (who emphasized that a picture was, above anything else, a plane surface covered with colors assembled in a certain order) and yet could also provide his canvas with the richest human, sexual, and even social implications and associations. He reveals and conceals, takes away and adds, seduces and soothes. This eclectic—who was aristocrat, socialist, and sensualist in one person—employs the devices of the Ivory Coast craftsmen, whose statues excite us aesthetically without moving us emotionally, and those of the Byzan-

tine and Early Renaissance icon-makers which touch us but cannot stir our depths, and, *e pluribus,* shapes a "Modigliani" that is pulsating, breathing, living—though anyone a little less gifted, a little less ardent, would have ended up as a maker of pastiches!

There is more in a picture of Modigliani—like El Greco, that earlier Mannerist—than meets the impatient eye. A quick glance takes in the superficial characteristics by which anyone believes he can spot a Modigliani from a distance: the flat, mask-like face; the almond-shaped eyes; the spatulate or slightly twisted nose; the pursed, small mouth; all of it in a head thinned out to the extreme; the neck either overlong or virtually nonexistent; the calculated disproportion between head, torso, and leg; the sculptural approach (maintained despite the artist's total indifference to light, shade, and atmosphere); and, finally, the resonant and intensely luminous, yet uncomplicated color, applied with an accuracy that is totally absent in most other Expressionists, especially Soutine.

Yet if one gives more than a fleeting glance to a Modigliani, its intrinsic Expressionism—checked, to be sure, by that element of aristocratic restraint likely to be found among urban Tuscans—will come to the surface. The frequent complaint that all Modiglianis look alike fades as one begins to study his work with some of the earnestness with which it was composed. The men and women whose countenances appear in his work—Lipchitz, Soutine, Rivera, and Picasso, the poet Jean Cocteau, the sculptor Henri Laurens, the artist's companions Beatrice Hastings and Jeanne Hébuterne, and others about whom we know less or even nothing, including some who belong to the so-called dregs of society—are characterized in the most subtle ways: by a stronger tilting of the head; a variation of the angle of the nose; an ironic, surly, or deeply sensitive mouth; the precise positioning of arms and hands; or by the arbitrary application of color, hot or cold to provide the desired mood. His sitters are elegant or slovenly, sensuous or dispassionate, intellectual or dull. All Modiglianis look no more alike than do all Chinese or Indians: after a little observation, striking physiognomic differences can be noted despite what in art language would be called "stylization".

Modigliani's nudes are in a way the least "sexy" ones ever painted, and yet they are enormously seductive to anyone who can fathom the excitement that made these transfigurations of ordinary bodies into chromatic poems, sinuous red and ocher arabesques of frail limbs and high waists. Perhaps the police official who in 1918 had the nudes removed from the window of the Berthe Weill Gallery in Paris (during the only, and far from successful, one-man show the artist ever had in his lifetime) was prompted to this action not so much by the unusual display of pubic hair as by his vague sense that these unnaturalistic nudes exuded far more sexuality than the anatomically correct female nudes painted, say, by the celebrated academician Bouguereau. In the United States, the postal authorities demanded that the Guggenheim Museum withdraw from sale postcards showing Modigliani's *Nu Couché*. A *Life* magazine article on Modigliani brought in many letters of protest, one of which ended: "Nothing prevents me from ripping the dirt from the pages of your magazine before such 'art' inspires my children." All these demonstrations merely indicate that Modigliani succeeded in filling his works with life and zest. Sir Kenneth Clark, in his book *The Nude,* formulates the justification when he writes: "No nude, however abstract, should fail to arouse in the spectator some vestige of erotic feeling . . . and if it does not do so, it is bad art and false morals."

"Ethics" might have been an even better word, for "morals" refers to society's generally accepted customs of conduct, whereas "ethics" distinguishes between the truly good and bad. Modigliani's nudes are devoid of the hypocrisy of Bouguereau, who gave his pictures a tincture of lewdness under the invisible but omnipresent mantle of respectability. Modigliani had high ethical principles, both as an artist and as a man. None of the many memoirs ever recall an occasion when this most excitable and often irascible man ever committed a mean act.

His work is full of compassion for man and the condition of a man, yet says neither too little nor too much; it has an amazing poise; it has melody; and it has a haunting quality of tenderness, of calm beauty. It is delicate, yet it also has strength. This is particularly evident in the drawings—mostly done with a fine pencil—in which the undulating sharp line has an imperious assurance that makes the spectator fill in wherever the contour may omit a section of face or body.

His art is fraught with mystery, often achieved by a simple device—by either closing the "window of the soul" or indicating the eye as just a narrow brow or brown slit. Is this elision of the eye meant to keep out the hostile world, to foster concentration upon oneself? Did the introspective artist, toward the end of his life, come to feel that it was as preposterous to paint an eye as to try to render the sun? Was he aware of the fast-approaching end, which might hold nothing beyond?

Perhaps he knew all he had to know when, as he was taken to the Hôpital de la Charité, he remarked to a friend about Jeanne and himself, "We're sure of eternal happiness, she and I, whatever happens." Perhaps these slits in the place of naturalistic eyes are the narrow openings to an inner world that the Expressionist Modigliani sought and saw beneath the phenomena of mortal things.

I have only indicated once, in passing, that in addition to drawings and paintings, Modigliani also produced sculpture. In *Die Kunst des 20ten Jahrhunderts,* Carl Einstein drew attention to it as early as 1926. Still, to nine out of ten art lovers, Modigliani's ventures into the realm of three-dimensional art have remained unknown. His gifts in this medium were highly appreciated only by some of his colleagues. In 1909, the British painter Augustus John visited Modigliani in his studio in Montmartre. The floor was "covered with statues, all much alike and prodigiously long and narrow." John, who bought a couple of them, wrote in his autobiography *Chiaroscuro:*

"The stone heads affected me deeply. For some days afterwards I found myself under the hallucination of meeting people in the street who might have posed for them, and that without myself resorting to the Indian Herb. Can 'Modi' have discovered a new and secret aspect of 'reality'?"

Those who have seen them have felt profoundly stirred by the glyptic works of Amedeo Modigliani. In them, the artist had created convincing aesthetic symbols of the new era. Nearly all his biographers pay tribute to his sculpture in a page or two, and writers, as well as artists, maintain that his superiority as a sculptor is above doubt, this in spite of the fact that his sculpture is only a small segment of his total *oeuvre,* since he devoted himself to sculpture for no more than one quarter of his brief career. But no comprehensive study of Modigliani's sculptures has appeared in print up to now, nor has an attempt been made before to locate and reproduce his surviving three-dimensional works. Twenty-five have been identified so far, including one or two whose authenticity is not unanimously upheld.

Not enough attention has been paid, indeed, to a very tragic detail of his career—the fact that he desperately wanted to be a sculptor and nothing else, and that, had not circumstances prevented the realization of his dream, we might have been blessed with a sculptor even more important as an artist than the superb painter Modigliani. To quote his contemporary, the dealer Adolphe Basler "Sculpture was his only ideal [*son unique idéal*] and he put high hopes in it." Nina Hamnett, who knew Modigliani, as she knew everybody in the artists' quarter, once summed up his predicament in a sentence:

"He always regarded sculpture as his real *métier,* and it was probably only lack of money, the difficulty of obtaining material, and the amount of time required to complete a work in stone that made him return to painting during the last five years of his life."

She omitted two additional obstacles. One was the artist's poor health: sculpture demanded a strength his frail body did not have, and, yielding to the doctor's order, he had to give up the hammer and chisel because his throat and lungs, delicate since the attack of tuberculosis he had suffered in his teens, were most adversely affected by the constant inhalation of the inevitable stone dust. Moreover, sculptures were difficult to exhibit, and, if not traditional, almost impossible to sell—a fact which even an idealist like Modigliani, whose requirements were unbelievably few, could not afford to overlook. A meal or a drink could be obtained, now and then, for a portrait drawing, and the untiring Zborowski could be relied upon to find an occasional buyer for one of his canvases.

After all this has been said, it would be logical to reclassify Modigliani, in homage to his feverish ambition, as a sculptor who also painted. But such a reclassification would be resisted by tradition and popular opinion. When, in 1945, Leon Gischia and Nicole Védrès published their book, *La Sculpture en France depuis Rodin,* Modigliani appeared in the section "La Sculpture des Peintres." In the bulletin *Musées de France* (December 1949), Bernard Dorival, director of the Musée National d'Art Moderne, proudly announcing the first acquisition of a sculpture by Modigliani, lists him in an article entitled "Sculpture de Peintres." He admits, in the same essay, that for Modigliani, unlike Matisse, La Fresnaye, or Braque, sculpture was not a secondary activity, but "*sa vocation même, l'art pour lequel il etait né.*"

In 1951, New York's Curt Valentin Gallery included Modigliani in an exhibition called "Sculpture by Painters," along with masters from Géricault and Daumier to André Masson and George L. K. Morris, and in 1958 he was presented in New York's Chalette Gallery, in an exhibition with the same title. Yet all the other artists in these shows were painters who considered sculpture as only a minor, perhaps even accidental, outlet for their creative vigor. It should also be borne in mind that some of the major men in this group, such as Matisse, Renoir, Braque and Degas, were modelers in clay or wax (including Picasso, though he did make some carvings, as well as constructions in metal, wood, and other materials). Painters prefer modeling in soft materials —perhaps because they are more used to working with tractable media-rather than the laborious use of mallet and chisel.

Oddly, and paradoxically, Modigliani, despite his extraordinarily high-strung temperament, preferred the rather slow process of direct carving. (However, in recent years, two bronzes have been attributed to him; unfortunately, the models from which they were cast have not been identified.) He had in common with most of the "painter-sculptors of his generation the preoccupation with the human figure. Modigliani, who, as far as we know, painted and carved human figures almost exclusively, could have said of himself with greater justification than did Matisse, the "King of the Fauves" (who, after all, painted many landscapes and still lifes):

"What interests me most is neither still life nor landscape but the human figure. It is through it that I best succeed in expressing the nearly religious feeling that I have toward life."

Although many people saw him joyously engrossed in the carving of stone, or remarked (as did Augustus John) upon the works in stone that were in evidence all over his dwellings, the chronology of these works is most uncertain, based as it is upon the vague recollections of his friends. A head, posthumously cast in bronze, whose authenticity has been questioned, has been dated as early as 1906; on the other hand, André Salmon affixed the equally improbable date of 1919 to one of the stone sculptures. The period 1909 to 1914, however, appears to have been the time when virtually all the pieces were produced. It is significant that Pfannstiel, in his catalogue of paintings, records only five oils in 1910, three in 1911, none in 1912, two in 1913, while no fewer than forty-four canvases of the next two years are identified. In the five years preceding the outbreak of the war, Modigliani must have been engaged chiefly in what Dorival was to call his "main passion." He seems to have been very contented, plunging himself deeply into work, often taking up his chisel when the first sunrays lit the studio, and laboring ceaselessly throughout the day.

The beginning of his sculptural career is shrouded in darkness. At the academies of Florence and Venice he did not, as far as we know, enroll in any sculpture class. If, during his trip at the. age of seventeen through some of Italy's major cities, he was greatly impressed by the sculptures he saw in churches and museums, the letters to his friend Ghiglia are silent about this fascination. All we know for sure is that, according to the painter de Zarate, Modigliani in 1902, "expressed a burning desire to become a sculptor and was deploring the cost of materials." De Zarate goes on:

"He was painting only *faute de mieux*. His real ambition was to work in stone, and this desire stayed with him during his whole life . . ."

The artist's daughter Jeanne also refers to a letter assigned to 1902 and addressed to a friend, Gino Romiti, which mentions Amedeo's sculptural activity at Pietrasanta, near Carrara (a region which he was to revisit years later). Subsequently, soon after his arrival in Paris in 1906, he confided to his first friend there, the Russian artist Granowski, his wish to create colossal monuments, works on the scale of Michelangelo's. Without a substantial work of his own to back his claim, he introduced himself as a sculptor to André Utter.

That in his formative years Modigliani was really drawn to the work of the Gothic sculptor Tino di Camaino, as is maintained by Jeanne Modigliani and the critic Enzo Carli, is open to doubt. Tino, who is only briefly mentioned by Vasari, and receives only three or four lines in Jacob Burckhardt's celebrated ninteenth-century guide to Italian art, *Der Cicerone*, was not fully appreciated before the twentieth century. If there are affinities betwen Tino's oblique placing of elongated heads on cylindrical necks and the manner of Modigliani, these can be due to conceptual similarities in styles tending toward the formal and abstract rather than to any precocious wisdom on the part of a very young man to whom we must not ascribe unusual powers of discernment. Modigliani's documented admiration for Domenico Morelli (creator of melodramatic paintings of Biblical subjects, historical events and scenes from Tasso, Shakespeare, and Byron) and the fact that, upon his arrival in Paris, he decorated his apartment with reproductions of works by Correggio, Andrea del Sarto, Titian, and other High Renaissance painters, leads one to suspect that young Modigliani had not yet acquired the sophistication needed to appreciate the Italian "Primitives."

Modigliani's aesthetic ripening began with an admiration for Toulouse-Lautrec and exposure to the work of Cézanne whose memorial show at the Salon d'Automne (1907) was an eye-opener to young artists. He knew, and held in high esteem, the aged Douanier, Henri Rousseau, and also Pablo Picasso, only three years older than himself but already on the way to becoming a *chef d' école*. Modigliani was introduced to the Fauves, the Cubists, and the Futurists, to Negro and Indo-

Chinese art—it is impossible that he missed any of the sensations to be had in the art world of Paris in the first decade of this century.

The aging Rodin, one must assume, was not among his idols. It cannot be said with certainty now whether his rejection of Rodin antedated his pivotal meeting, early in 1909, with Constantin Brancusi or whether it was during his long conversations with Brancusi that he became convinced that Rodin's influence was unfortunate. Brancusi, born in Roumania and eight years older than Modigliani had begun as an admirer of Rodin, but had turned away from the master, refused to become his assistant ("Nothing can grow under big trees!"), and developed a style of immaculate hardness diametrically opposed to Rodin's soft modeling. Blind to the greatness of Rodin's earlier work, Modigliani was contemptuous of the demigod. The bulk of Rodin's works are bronzes, and Modigliani disliked all modeling (the forming of a figure in a malleable material such as wax or clay). Nor could he have mustered up enthusiasm for the aging master's soapy marbles, cut, not by Rodin himself, but by his *metteurs au point* and *praticiens.*

In Paris, the century's first decade was most fertile in the realm of glyptic arts, if one recalls the names of Duchamps-Villon, Brancusi, Laurens, Nadelman, Archipenko and, the youngest of them, Lipchitz. Of these men, only Jacques Lipchitz was really close to Modigliani (though Lipchitz's art developed in a totally different direction). Brancusi, the purist and logician, who, through a process of extreme simplification, excluded everything not absolutely relevant to his purposes, was more mentor than friend. In some ways, Brancusi was the great rejuvenator of sculpture which around 1900 had deteriorated into a kind of three-dimensional painting. He was the very antithesis to Medardo Rosso, who wanted art to make the spectator forget the material, and even suggested that people should not walk around a statue any more than around a painting. From Brancusi, the disciple Modigliani was to learn the insistence on the integrity of the material, the importance of direct cutting, the emphasis on the essence of things as against a mere imitation of external surface. Before the two men met, Brancusi had carved the *Woman's Head,* a

perfect oval into which are incised near-abstract outlines of nose, eyes, and mouth, simple and intense. Here the modern trend of depersonalizaiton may be said to have started, the substitution of aesthetically pleasing form for psychological portraiture.

To judge by the drawings and paintings made prior to 1909, Modigliani, in whom the admiration for Toulouse-Lautrec had been replaced by a Cézanne worship, had unwittingly, prepared himself for the great encounter. Gradually, he evidences a higher and higher degree of plastic feeling, a solidity of form which allows no detachment of the parts of the body, an increasing tendency toward rhythm and simplification. Neither man has left written accounts of their meetings. But we have André Salmon's report:

"To Brancusi's studio on Rue Vaugirard . . . Modigliani came and went, his hands in the pockets of his everlasting velvet suit, clutching to his hip the ever present drawing pad bound in celestial blue . . . Brancusi gave no advice, gave no lessons. But from there, Modigliani took the idea of geometry in space, different from that which was usually taught, or which at that time could have been found in modern studios. Tempted by sculpture, he tried his hand, but retained from those days in Brancusi's studio only that lengthening of the human figure, which characterizes so directly the style of his painted figures."

The German critic Curt Stoermer met Modigliani in the same year, 1909, visiting him in his ground floor studio at 14 Cité Falguière (off Rue Vangirard just beyond the Boulevard Montparnasse):

"He had a tremendous urge to make sculptures himself. Having ordered a large piece of sandstone to be placed in his studio, he cut directly into the stone. Just as there were times when he loved idleness and indulged in it with the greatest sophistication, there were also times when he plunged himself deep into work. He cut all his sculptures directly into the stone, never touching clay or plaster. He felt destined to be a sculptor. There were certain periods when this urge started, and thrusting all painting tools aside, he snatched up the hammer."

The most detailed story comes from the dealer

and critic Adolphe Basler, who, oddly, does not mention Brancusi:

"Modigliani seemed to abandon painting [in 1909]. Negro sculpture haunted him and the art of Picasso tormented him. This was the time when the Polish sculptor Nadelman exhibited his works at the Druet Gallery. The Natanson brothers, former editors of the *Revue Blanche*, drew the attention of Gide and [Octave] Mirbeau to this new talent. The experiments of Nadelman also disturbed Picasso. In fact, the principles of spherical decomposition in Nadelman's drawings and sculptures preceded the subsequent experiments of the cubist Picasso. The sculptures of Nadelman which astonished Modigliani were a stimulus to him.[3] His curiosity turned to the forms created by the archaic Greeks, and to the Indo-Chinese (Khmer) sculpture that was beginning to be known among the painters and sculptors, and he assimilated much else besides, though he always reserved his admiration for the refined art of the Far East, and for the simplified proportions of Negro sculpture.

"For several years, Modigliani did nothing but draw, and trace round and supple arabesques, faintly emphasizing with a bluish or rosy tone the elegant contours of those numerous caryatids which he always planned to execute in stone. And he attained a design very sure, very melodious, at the same time with a personal accent, with great charm, sensitive and fresh. Then one day he started to sculpt figures and heads directly out of the stone. He used the chisel only until the war, but the few sculptures of his which remain reveal more than a little of his great aspirations. He tended toward restrained forms, but not entirely abstract in their schematic conciseness."

There were two fellow sculptors who met him somewhat later than the men quoted so far, and while they admired his talent, they were not blind to his foibles. One of these was Ossip Zadkine, who knew Modigliani after he had got himself a studio at 216 Boulevard Raspail, where he devoted himself almost exclusively to sculpture. Zadkine regretfully says that Modigliani allowed himself to be too sketchy in his work. His statues were "never finished, as though for shame, not for a mysterious reason." Zadkine also saw him make painted sculptures (*sculptures poly-*

chromes), of which not a single one is extant. Eventually he noticed that Modigliani was slackening his efforts: "Little by little the sculptor in him was dying."

Zadkine remembered Modigliani wearing a freshly laundered corduroy suit: "He looked like a young god disguised as a workman out in his Sunday best." The painter Tsugouharu Foujita, who met Modigliani at the end of 1913, also mentioned the corduroy suit, as well as the checked shirts and the red belt he wore. From Foujita we gain a touching impression of Modigliani as a young Bohemian, his hair usually tousled, making sketches—since he had no money—of people who bought him Pernod. Foujita also remembers Modigliani as being fond of poetry, especially Tagore, and much interested in the art of China and Japan.

Another friend was Jacob Epstein, who talked warmly about him to Arnold Haskell. After mentioning Degas, Epstein continued:

"Modigliani is another case of the modern painter-sculptor. At one period, he produced some exceedingly interesting carvings with curiously elongated faces and thin, razor-like noses that would often break off and have to be stuck on again. He would buy a block of ordinary stone for a few francs from a mason engaged on a building and wheel it back to his studio in a barrow. He was influenced by Negro art but in no way dominated by it. He had a vision entirely his own and people are wrong when they call him imitative. It is, of course, as a painter that he is known, but he would also have excelled as a sculptor. Many of his drawings are entirely sculpturesque in conception and design" (Arnold Haskell, *The Sculptor Speaks*).

In his autobiography, *Let There Be Sculpture*, Epstein came back to Modigliani. He recalled that his studio ("a miserable hole within a courtyard") was filled with nine or ten long heads, and one figure: "At night he would place candles on the top of each one and the effect was that of a primitive temple. A legend of the quarter said that Modigliani, when under the influence of hashish, embraced these sculptures." (A former sweetheart recalled that she and Modigliani often had supper by the light of a guttering candle fixed to the top of the very head that is now in the Tate Gallery.)

Jacques Lipchitz has given us a full report on his late friend:

"The first time we met was when Max Jacob [the poet-painter] introduced me to him, and Modigliani invited me to his studio at the Cité Falguière. At that time [in 1913] he was making sculpture, and of course I was especially interested to see what he was doing.

"When I came to his studio—it was spring or summer—I found him working outdoors. A few heads in stone—maybe five—were standing on the cement floor of the court in front of the studio. He was adjusting them one next to the other.

"I can see him as if it were today, stooping over those heads of his, explaining to me that he had conceived all of them as an ensemble. It seems to me that these heads were exhibited later the same year in the Salon d'Automne, arranged in step-wise fashion, like tubes of an organ, to produce the special music he wanted.[4]

"Modigliani, like some others at the time, was very taken with the notion that sculpture was sick, that it had become very sick with Rodin and his influence. There was too much modeling in clay, too much 'mud.' The only way to save sculpture was to begin carving again, directly in stone. We had many very heated discussions about this, for I did not for one moment believe that sculpture was sick, nor did I believe that direct carving was by itself a solution to anything. But Modigliani could not be budged; he held firmly to his deep conviction. He had been seeing a good deal of Brancusi, who lived nearby, and he had come under his influence. When we talked of different kinds of stone—hard and soft—Modigliani said that the stone itself made very little difference; the important thing was to give the carved stone the feeling of hardness, and that came from within the sculptor himself; regardless of what stone they use, some sculptors make their work look soft, but others can use even the softest of stones and give their sculpture hardness. Indeed, his own sculpture shows how he used this idea."

Then Lipchitz adds:

"He could never forget his interest in people, and he painted them, so to say, with abandon,

urged on by the intensity of his feeling and vision. This is why Modigliani, though he admired African Negro and other primitive arts as much as any of us, was never profoundly influenced by them—any more than he was by Cubism. He took from them certain stylistic traits, but he was hardly affected by their spirit."

Lipchitz sheds no light on Modigliani's trip to Italy, an unsuccessful attempt to establish himself as a sculptor in Carrara (near the place where he had worked briefly as a youth). This attempt was made, according to the latest research in 1912, before the two men had met. Pfannstiel, Douglas, and Claude Roy mistakenly placed Modigliani's journey to Carrara in the year 1909, when Modigliani did indeed go to Italy to visit his family, but seems to have done only some painting (the *Beggar of Leghorn* is the sole finished product of his trip, according to Pfannstiel). It appears now that the story told by Douglas—that Modigliani was found emaciated and unconscious, lying on the floor in an abandoned studio in Montmartre, and that several friends collected money to send him back to his family for recovery—must refer to the summer of 1912. Emmanuele Modigliani gave his younger brother money to go and look for a studio near Carrara but the artist quickly returned to Leghorn, discouraged by the heat and by the difficulty of working the hard marble. In Leghorn in 1912 he did produce a number of sculptures, but was, according to reports, sneered at by friends who advised him to throw them in the nearest canal rather than to try to store them away. Jeanne Modigliani leaves us in doubt as to whether the artist followed this advice or, after all, took his works back to Paris. But Claude Roy maintains that Modigliani, in a mood of iconoclastic despair, actually loaded a handcart, then pushed the cart to the nearest canal, into which he dumped his sculptures. The scholar expresses the hope that "some archaeologically minded frogman will one day go in search of them, and restore them to their place in the sun."

Modigliani returned to Paris, to his work as well as to his old addictions. He seems to have continued sculpturing until the outbreak of World War I. There is no reason to believe that he was active in sculpture during the last five years of his tumultuous life. His physical condition permitted the continuation of painting, but sculpture was definitely out of the question. It was in those last five years that most of the paintings were produced!

It is unknown how many sculptures were actually done by the artist (even as late as 1960 a French critic estimated that no more than six or seven had survived), but the twenty-five that have been definitely identified undoubtedly constitute only a fraction of his output. Modigliani was known to destroy or discard all works that he considered below his standard. In addition, many of his works in all media were lost whenever, unable to pay the rent, he would slip out like a thief, leaving his creations to the mercy of the irate landlord. The stone Caryatid had a strange fate. It had been carved from a building stone found by the artist on the Boulevard Montparnasse, near a half-completed structure that had been abandoned when the workmen had been called up for military service in 1914. This piece was pushed over and broken. Later, upon the request of the architect Pierre Chareau, it was mended without alteration by Lipchitz, and it stood in the architect's garden until 1939. In that year it was shipped to an exhibition in San Francisco and it remained in the United States. It was shown again by the Museum of Modern Art in its Modigliani exhibition of 1951, and then acquired for its permanent collection.

The statues that have survived are of uneven value, and in various stages of completion, from mere sketches to completed works. As a rule they are cut out of limestone,[5] and they range in height from small heads, about twenty inches high, to the large standing figure (sixty-three inchs high) now in the collection of Gustav Schindler. Ten of the sculptures are in museums in England, France, and the United States, and more than a dozen are privately owned, mainly by Americans and Frenchmen.

The artist's place in the realm of modern sculpture is difficult to define. He does not fit into any of the schools that flourished around 1910, especially Cubism and Futurism. As said before, he was strongly influenced by Brancusi, whose work relies on surface sensousness, linear rhythm, and the relation of masses. But he went his own way. Whereas the Roumanian gradually turned from the human figure to find inspiration in seals, turtles, birds, and fish, Modigliani never abandoned the human motif, and, within the world of human beings, retained a much larger measure of recognizable affinity to nature than did his mentor.

The greatest influence on Modigliani, next to that of Brancusi, undoubtedly was exterted by African Negro art. Until sixty years ago, only ethnologists paid much attention to what were considered hideous little pagan idols. Around 1905, artists were the first to recognize in these wood carvings and bronzes some solutions they themselves were seeking to plastic problems. In Germany, young Ernst Ludwig Kirchner made his discoveries at Dresden's Ethnological Museum. In Paris, Vlaminck paid a few sous for an African statue he had found lying about in a local bistro—probably left there by a sailor, as a souvenir—and took it to his friend Derain. "Nearly as beautiful as the Venus of Milo, isn't it?" "Quite as beautiful," said Derain. They showed it to Picasso, whose verdict was, "More beautiful!"

Modigliani saw samples of African Negro art in the shop of the dealer Joseph Brummer, and also in the collection of the painter Frank Burty-Haviland. To judge by his own sculptures, he was particularly impressed by works from the Ivory Coast, a prosperous and highly civilized region. Some of the Baule masks and other pieces, with their long, domed, flat noses, the joining of the line of nose and eyelids and the almond shape of the eyes, resemble the Italian's work. The mouth is the same narrow short slit, and there is the same stylized coiffure.

The aspects he himself was seeking—the new feeling for form, the tranquility and equilibrium —must have appealed to him. There was no action, no emotion, no character, incident, or story, yet a mood of mystery emanated from these subtle combinations of geometrical forms, in contrapuntal application, where majesty and greatness were achieved in a way reminiscent of ancient Egyptian or archaic Greek sculptures. Here, at last, anonymous "barbaric" craftsmen showed how perfect, rhythmically balanced form could be attained by creating in conceptual rather than purely visual terms; how abstract and conventionalized selectivity captured dignity and serenity that often escaped the artist who aimed for illusionistic reality. Here was perfection in the elegant and precise rendering of surface planes and details, an architectonic equilibrium of mass that was missing in many works of celebrated Beaux-Arts professors.

The origin of these pieces was largely religious and thus "utilitarian"; these craftsmen were probably unaware of producing art in the sense the term is used in modern Europe. However, in conversation Modigliani maintained that these sculptures were consciously produced works of art in the fullest sense of the term rather than mere fetishes. *L'art nègre* helped Modigliani to find his own solutions.[6] Just as the Negro artist, limited to a few motifs and conventionalized in certain directions, was able to use his creative abilities on problems of pure form, organization, and design, so Modigliani, not caring about originality, literary ideas, or the demands of naturalism, now could treat his few themes with the utmost intellectual clarity.

Undoubtedly, Modigliani looked at Khmer art which was being discovered, and also at archaic Greek and Romanesque art. But Negro art was and remained the strongest influence. It is true that Modigliani's sculptures display a strong Western classical element. But it must be born in mind that African art is also "classical"—as has been pointed out—as opposed to romantic art (*vide* Rodin) in which the artist is mainly eager to express his individual, personal, "original" vision.[7]

However great this influence of Negro art, one must not make the mistake of declaring Modigliani's sculptures to be imitations of West African art. It had about the same effect on him that, decades earlier, Hokusai's color prints had had on Manet. In either case, the European artist excitedly saw the exotic artist's omissions, distortions, and exaggerations, and made a mental note of them. Pfannstiel was right in rejecting the suggestion that Modigliani's work had taken on

any African characteristics (as did Picasso's, for a while). A decade later, in 1938, Robert J. Goldwater demonstrated in detail why, whatever inspirations Modigliani may have gotten by looking at African sculptures, his work is quite original:

Though he keeps the long neck that we have noticed Picasso omitting, he bends and curves it, as he tilts the head, in order to continue the arabesques of the sloping shoulders; the oval eyes are tilted, and the long nose becomes concave in outline. In his flat forms Modigliani never achieves any of the effect of cubic mass that is supposed to be the main influence of Negro art, and even his sentimental linear rhythms are far removed from the repetitions of design on which African sculpture is built. In accordance with the decorative character of his whole art his deformations of form are elongations adding to grace and sentiment, and so are directly opposed to the thickening of mass characteristics of Negro sculpture."

Goldwater observes that even in those samples of Modigliani's sculptural art where the affinity to African art seems greatest, there are as many differences as there are similiarities.[8] The faces are rectangular in either case, the mouths narrow short slits, the noses long and flat, and joined in one line with the eyelids. The mouth as fashioned by Modigliani, slightly twisted upward, is put close under the nose, whereas the Dance Mask, to which Goldwater compares a typical Modigliani head, has the mouth down near the bottom of the chin. Altogether, there is nothing frighteningly deathlike about Modigliani's works, which are generally serene and lovely in their androgynous complexity.

Therefore, we should not overlook the Western sources that may have inspired the young sculptor. One should not forget his Italian origin and the fact that he was, during his formative years, exposed to Greek and Roman as well as Italian Renaissance works, plentifully exhibited in Florence, Rome, Naples, Venice and other cities he visited. Well read as he was, he surely must have known Michelangelo's famous letter to Messer Benedetto, containing important statements on the relationship between sculpture and painting:

"It seems to me," wrote Michelangelo, "that the nearer painting approaches sculpture the better

XXV

it is, and that sculpture is worse the nearer it approaches painting . . . By sculpture I mean that which is done by carving—sculpture that is done by adding on resembles painting."

To escape the influence of Rodin, many sculptors in the period between 1900 and 1910 turned to the world of antiquity. Nadelman went to the Glyptothek in Munich with its collection of fifth-century pediment figures from the temple of Aegina. Modigliani's work, however, has stronger affinities with the archaic period of Greek art, which was not much concerned with naturalistic representation, but more occupied with formal patterns. Like the archaic Greek sculptors (and like early Egyptian masters), Modigliani bore in mind the strong affinity between architecture and sculpture. Whereas a great deal of nineteenth-century sculpture is quite independent of its surroundings, and can be used in a garden corner or on a table as decoration, Modigliani's works have retained the architectural strength found in the figures that were inalienable parts of ancient buildings (there are even, in a few of them, architectural fragments behind or above the head[9]). While in the Victorian era much of sculpture deteriorated into pathetic bric-à-brac (often blown up to huge size), Modigliani's work is reminiscent of the sculptured figures called upon to serve within the massive framework of an Aegean sanctuary.[10] This is particularly evident if one looks at the large female figure (owned by Gustav Schindler) and at the somewhat smaller Caryatid. We know, in fact, that Modigliani dreamed of producing a great series of stone caryatids—possibly hundreds of them—which he called "*colonnes de tendresse*" (pillars of tenderness). They were supposed to surround his Temple of Beauty, a Temple dedicated to the glory of Man rather than God. But except for the one Caryatid now in New York's Museum of Modern Art, all that he managed to create was a large number of preliminary sketches—in gouache, pencil, crayon, water color—of such figures designed to serve as architectural columns. They differ from his portrait drawings. In the first place, they are chiefly frontal, and they occupy a definite amount of space (like a niche), thus indicating that the artist had a piece of sculpture in mind. Secondly, there is often more than just a contour, inflections

suggesting disappearing planes and thus three-dimensional solidity. Thirdly, there is no psychological depth (as there is in most portraits by his hand); instead, we have quiet, hieratic anonymity, appropriate to the purpose.

In Greek architecture, and in the imitations of Renaissance and post-Renaissance Europe, caryatids taking the place of pillars, serve to uphold entablatures of roofs. The sculptor Aristide Maillol, seeing for the first time the caryatids of the Erechtheum in Athens, was so intoxicated by their beauty that the guards stationed there found it difficult to prevent him from climbing up to embrace them. Whereas these and other caryatids attached to buildings are in standing positions, Modigliani's sole sculptured caryatid and the caryatids he sketched on paper are all in a crouching position. Her eyes cast down, his female roof-bearer always supports the heavy weight above her on her two extended arms, sometimes held sidewise, sometimes one on each side of the head, raised like brackets".

After Modigliani gave up sculpture, he produced more than two hundred paintings. The lessons he learned while concentrating on sculpture were not wasted, and they clearly enhanced the formal strength and structural solidity of his painting, as if to echo the words uttered by the artist's compatriot, Michelangelo: "It seems to me that the nearer painting approaches sculpture, the better it is . . ." Michelangelo was, of course, as biased about sculpture (which he placed high above painting) as was his antagonist, Da Vinci (who claimed that sculptors lacked intelligence). It is not necessary for painting (which deals with flat surfaces) to imitate sculpture. Oddly, Michelangelo, in practice, while the most sculptural of painters, was also the most "painterly" of sculptors, whereas the drawings and paintings of his "disciple" Modigliani show the same feeling for plasticity that, as a sculptor, he managed to achieve with an astonishing economy of means.

Modigliani's paintings and drawings must never deflect our attention from the work that was Modigliani's "main passion." If the present volume enables art lovers to look long and earnestly at the often sad and melancholy, yet always hypnotizingly spiritual images he formed through the simplest combination of basic stereometric shapes, then the efforts of the publishers and of all those who aided the writer in the difficult task of assembling the scattered pictorial material and biographical evidence will not have been in vain.

Classically firm, never cold; wise, but not over-intellectual; representational and abstract at the same time, these haunting stone figures are certainly the most complete and perfect aesthetic transfigurations of Modigliani's inner imagery.

ALFRED WERNER

Footnotes

[1] The painter Moise Kisling and another friend tried to take Modigliani's death mask, but not being sculptors, they were inadequate to the task, and secured the help of Jacques Lipchitz. The mask exudes a serenity and repose that Modigliani seems to have lacked completely in life.

[2] Before Brancusi, Picasso may have meant most to Modigliani, though the Spaniard was only three years older and had, so far, produced barely more than a half dozen pieces of sculpture. "Picasso would give it a kick if he saw it," Modigliani said to a visitor, Louis Latourette, who had come to his Montmartre studio and admired the torso of an actress. "That's only a misfire," Modigliani explained, and added:

"One should judge without sentimentality. After all, that's only to begin again in another and better way. In any case, I've half a mind to chuck painting altogether and stick to sculpture, which I prefer."

[3] But according to Jeanne Modigliani, her father did not discover Nadelman's sculpture until 1913 (at the second one-man show at the Galerie Druet).

[4] Lipchitz erred only insofar as several stone heads—not necessarily identical with those he saw—were exhibited in 1912, in the tenth Salon. The catalogue lists seven heads ("a decorative ensemble") by Modigliani. A year earlier, Modigliani had shown several sculptures at the studio of his Portuguese-born painter-friend Amedeo de Suza Cardoso, on Rue du Colonel Combes.

[5] A small marble head is owned by Jean Masurel in Roubaix, France. Most other extant stone carvings by Modigliani are made of limestone such as the Pierre d'Euville which is quarried near a small town in eastern France, south of Verdun (it has a sandy or granular appearance, generally gray to buff colored, and is softer and easier to carve than marble, but, because of its physical structure which is less compact than that of marble, it does not take a high polish). He liked to obtain stones shaped like columns or pillars, and always retained the original form of the stone into which he would hew or scratch the significant details. At one point Modigliani turned to wood, probably to avoid the unpleasant phys-ical effects he suffered from working in stone. To obtain this wood, he is said to have stolen, with the aid of a painter friend, railroad ties from a nearby Métro station. Douglas must have seen several of the wood carvings, for he writes that all were "exactly of the dimensions of railway crossties." With the exception of the one sold at auction in 1951 and reproduced in this book, they have disappeared. They shared the fate of the *sculptures polychromes* mentioned by Zadkine. One also wonders what to make of a recollection, to be found in *From Renoir to Picasso,* by Michel Georges-Michel:

"In the gardens of a big industrialist on the Riviera, I saw a number of admirable statues by Modigliani, and, among others, one that he had carved for his own tomb and that of his wife . . ." There is no additional information to be found anywhere!

Once Modigliani, as was his habit, helped himself to a stone in a building lot one evening after the laborers had gone home. He worked on it for hours, then, leaving his sculpture half-finished, returned home. When he came back the next morning, the statue had disappeared—it had somehow been incorporated into the building.

[6] We know now that many tribes had real, professional artists (see *Africa: The Art of the Negro Peoples,* by Elsy Leuzinger). The affinity between Modigliani's art and Negro sculpture is now generally accepted. When, in April 1951, Perls Galleries in New York hung drawings by Modigliani alongside masks and figures from the Ivory Coast, valuable light was shed on the formation of Modigliani's style.

[7] If Modigliani ever had formulated his ideas in writing, they could have been almost identical with those expressed by a younger contemporary, the American John B. Flannagan, who wrote as follows: "To that instrument of the subconscious, the hand of the sculptor, there exists an image within every rock. The creative act of realization merely frees it . . ." According to Flannagan, the sculptor's goal is " . . . the austere elimination of the accidental for ordered simplification . . . the greatest possible preservation of cubic compactness . . . even to preserve the identity of the original rock so that it hardly seems carved."

8 James Johnson Sweeney also cautions us against over-estimating the Parisian artists' borrowings from Africans: "These [borrowings], like the adoption of characteristically negroid form-motifs by Modigliani . . . appear today as having been more in the nature of attempts at interpretation, or expressions of critical appreciation, than true assimilation. When we occasionally come across something in contemporary art that looks as if it might have grown out of a genuine plastic assimilation of the Negro approach, on closer examination we almost invariably find that it can as fairly be attributed to another influence nearer home."

9 Occasionally, the view was expressed that the heads, or at least some of them, were intended as door jambs or mantelpiece pillars. The Head that is now in the Tate Gallery, was known, while it was owned and displayed by London's Victoria and Albert Museum, as "Head for the Top of a Door Jamb," because it was held that it had been intended to decorate the upper part of a door, with the lintel resting directly upon it.

10 Other periods and examples of art as well have been drawn into the orbit by art critics. R. S. Wilenski, contemplating the figure now in the Tate Gallery, was reminded of forms in medieval sculpture influenced by Byzantine manuscripts, as well as of Chinese Tang figures. Dorival compares one of Modigliani's heads acquired by the Musée d'Art Moderne, with certain Eastern Asiatic Buddhas, as well as with twelfth-century works by Langue d'Oc, and sculptures on the Porte Royale of the Cathedral of Chartres. He sees in it the spirituality of an El Greco, and the Mannerist technique of certain Tuscan Renaissance artists. These comments only show that there must exist a spiritual kinship between the plastic forms of all ages and nations, and that the best masters, whatever their origin, always considered emotional fervor, full three-dimensional realization, and truth to material more important than representational accuracy.

11 Concerning Modigliani's caryatids, Bernard Dorival wrote: "Few themes have . . . haunted the artist's mind so much." He might have added: "and long after he had abandoned sculpture, indeed, to his very end." The American writer Frederick S. Wight remarks: "He was obsessed by a theme for sculpture; to Modigliani it was what the reclining figure is to Henry Moore." He then asks: "This crouching figure designed to carry weight—was it an image of a mother who supported him?" However, Signora Eugenia Modigliani does not come to mind as much as does the extremely stylized, abbreviated, sphinx-like face of Brancusi's Mlle. Pogany.

Selected Bibliography

Adam, Leonard, *Primitive Art* (London, 1949)

Basler, Adolphe, *La Sculpture Moderne* (Paris, 1928)

Dorival, Bernard, "Musée d'Art Moderne. Sculpture de Peintres," Bulletin, *Musées de France* (Paris, December 1949)

"Trois Oeuvres de Modigliani," *ibidem* (Paris, September 1950)

Douglas, Charles, *Artist Quarter* (London, 1941)

Flannagan, John B., catalogue, Museum of Modern Art (New York, 1942)

Giedion-Welcker, Carola, *Contemporary Sculpture,* a revised and enlarged edition (New York, 1960)

Gischia, Léon and Védrès, Nicole, *La Sculpture en France depuis Rodin* (Paris, 1945)

Goldwater, Robert J., *Primitivism in Modern Art* (New York, 1938)

Jedlicka, Gotthard, *Modigliani* (Erlenbach-Zurich, 1953)

Leuzinger, Elsy, *Africa: The Art of The Negro Peoples* (New York, 1961)

Lipchitz, Jacques, *Modigliani* (New York, 1951)

Meidner, Ludwig, "Young Modigliani," *Burlington Magazine* (London, April 1942)

Modigliani, Jeanne, *Modigliani, Man and Myth* (New York, 1958)

Modigliani number, *Paris Montparnasse* (Paris, February 1930), with contributions by Adolphe Basler, André Salmon, Ossip Zadkine and others.

Modigliani, Preface by Maud Dale (New York, 1929)

Pfannstiel, Arthur, *Modigliani*, with a preface by Louis Latourette (Paris, 1929)

Modigliani et son Oeuvre (Paris, 1956)

Raynal, Maurice, *Modern French Painters* (New York, 1929)

Roy, Claude, *Modigliani* (New York, 1958)

Russoli, Franco, *Modigliani* (New York, n.d.)

Salmon, André, *Modigliani, Sa Vie et son Oeuvre* (Paris 1926)

Scheiwiller, Giovanni, *Amedeo Modigliani* (Zurich, 1958)

Sculpture by Painters, catalogue, Curt Valentin Gallery (New York, 1951)

Seuphor, Michele, *The Sculpture of this Century* (New York, 1960)

Stoermer, Curt, "Erinnerungen an Modigliani," *Der Querschnitt* (Berlin, June 1931)

Sweeney, James Johnson, *African Negro Art* (New York, 1935)

Vitali, Lamberto, ed., *Forty-Five Drawings by Modigliani* (New York, n.d.)

Werner, Alfred, "Modigliani as a Sculptor," *Art Journal* New York, winter 1960-61)

Wilenski, Reginald H., *The Meaning of Modern Sculpture* (London, 1935)

While Modigliani's paintings can be dated with a modicum of certainty, no definite chronology can be established for his sculpture and drawings. We know only that the sculpture was produced between 1909 and 1915. Modigliani did not date his works and did not refer to them specifically in his letters. Although dealers and friends of the artist have sometimes suggested putative dates, these dates are omitted here for lack of documentary proof. In many cases different authorities have proposed different dates for the same works. Dimensions are given except where it proved impossible to obtain them.

1

5

6

10

11

14

23

24

34

41

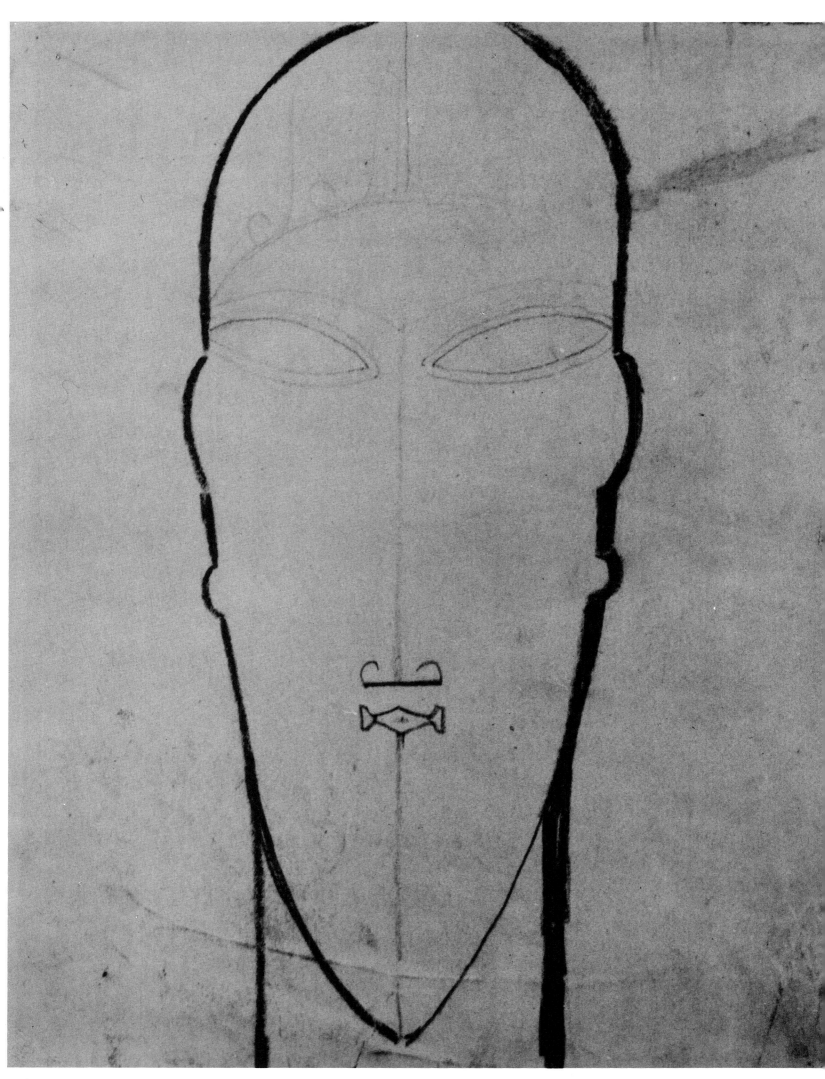

56

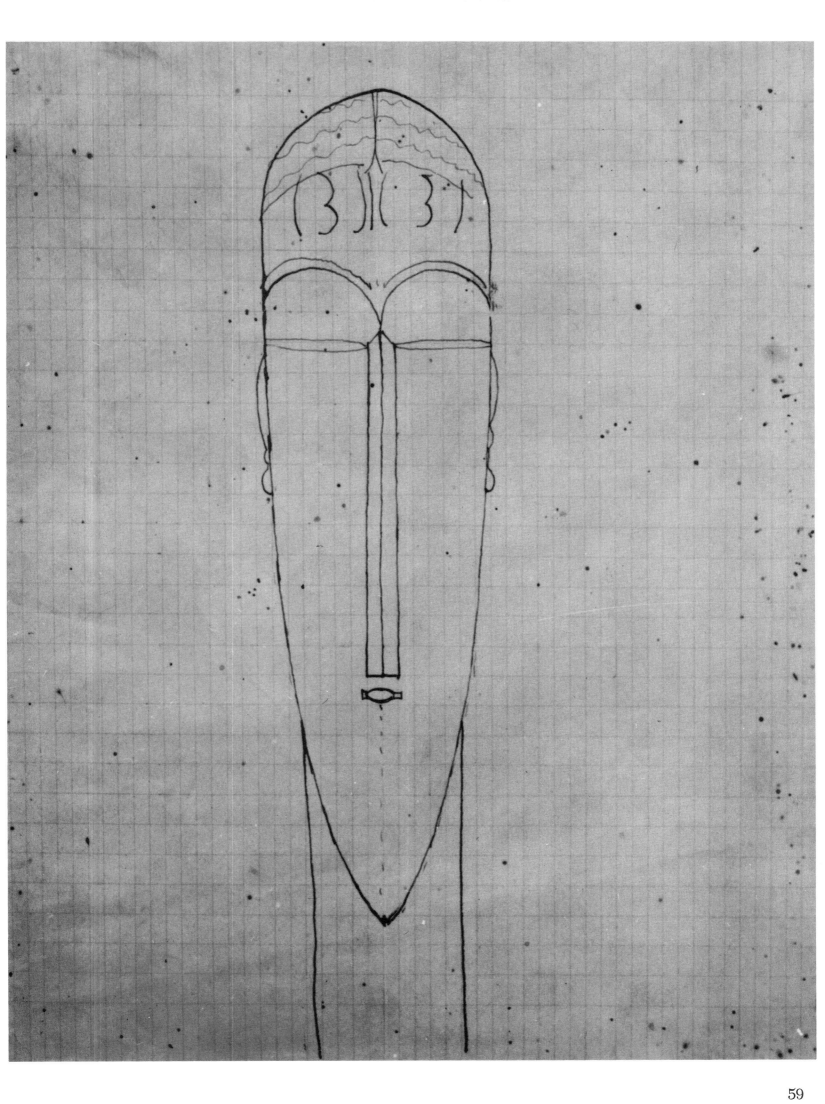

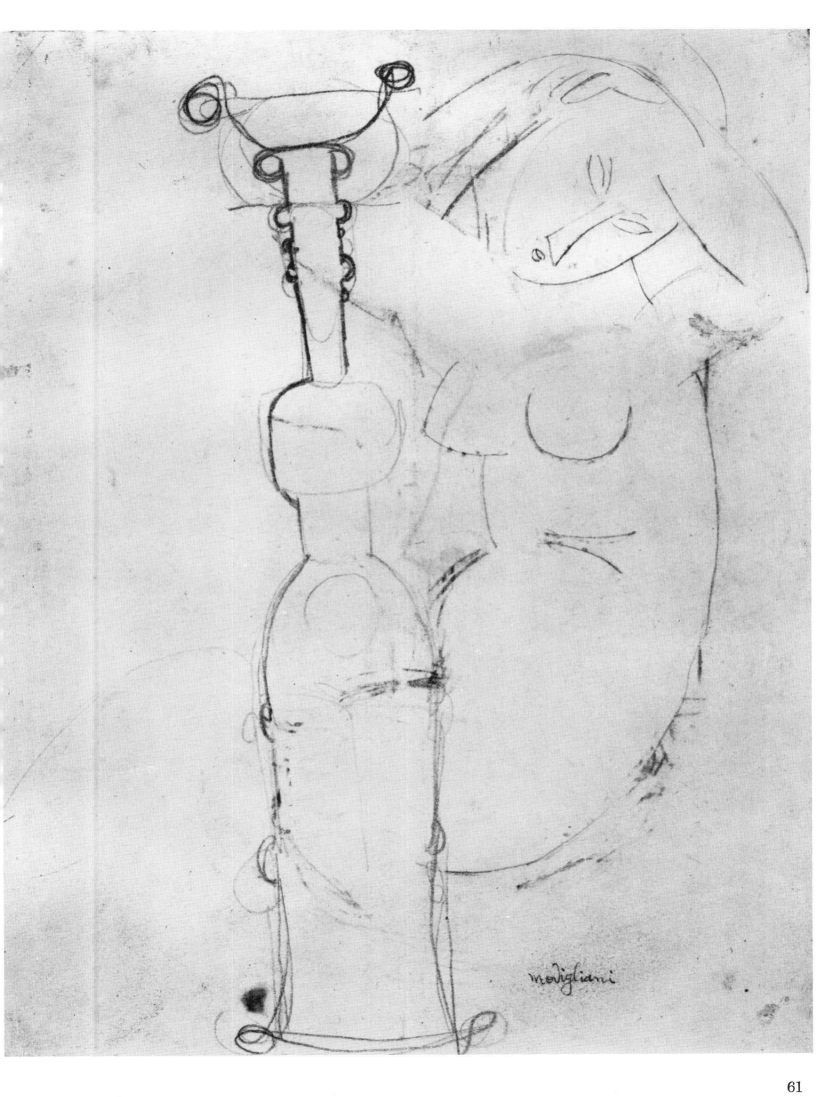

64

65

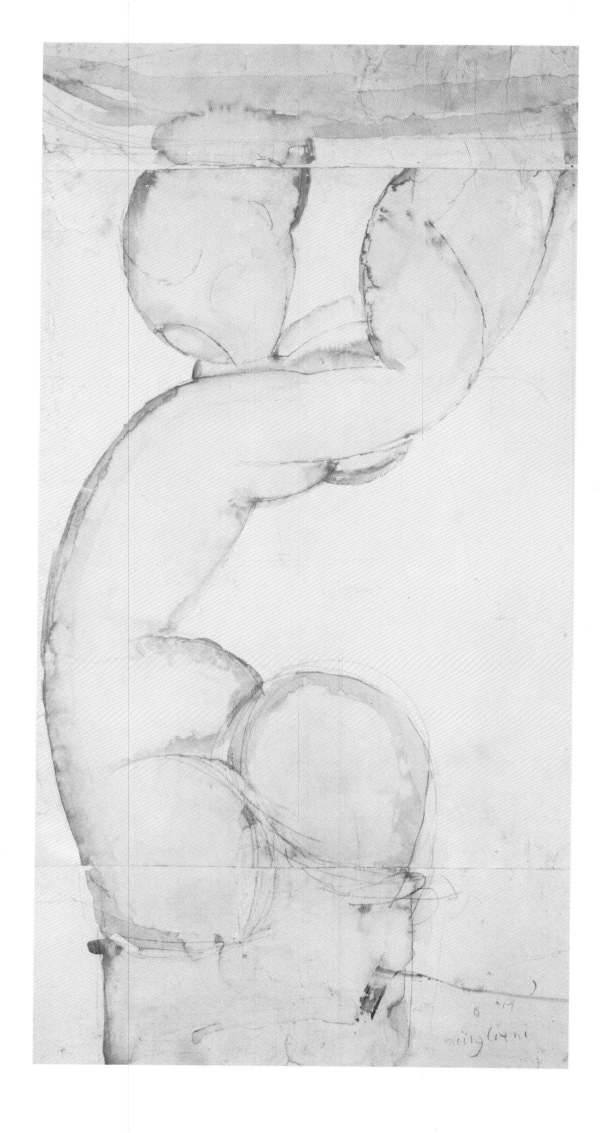

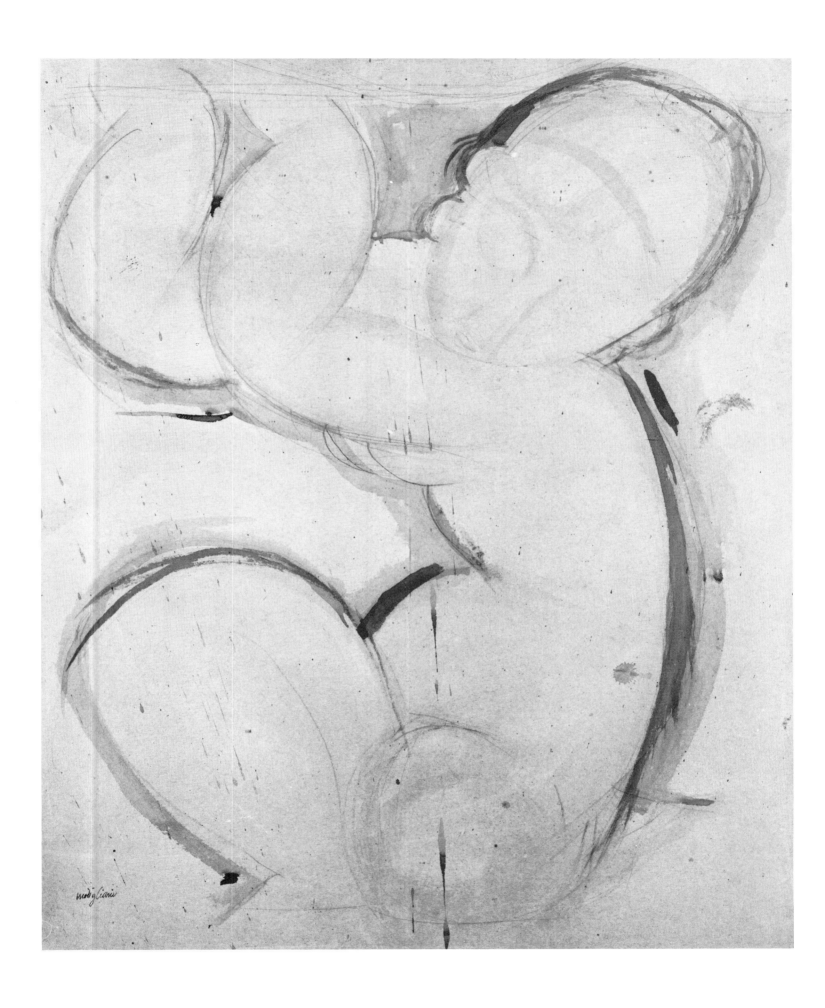

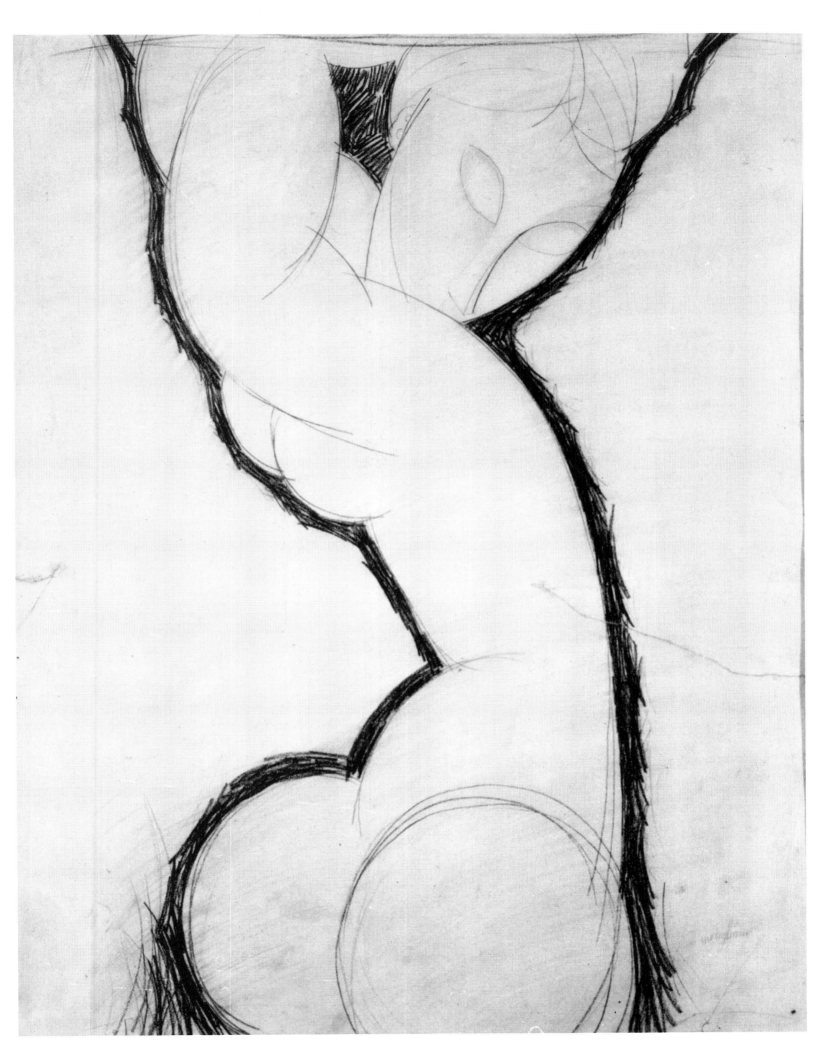

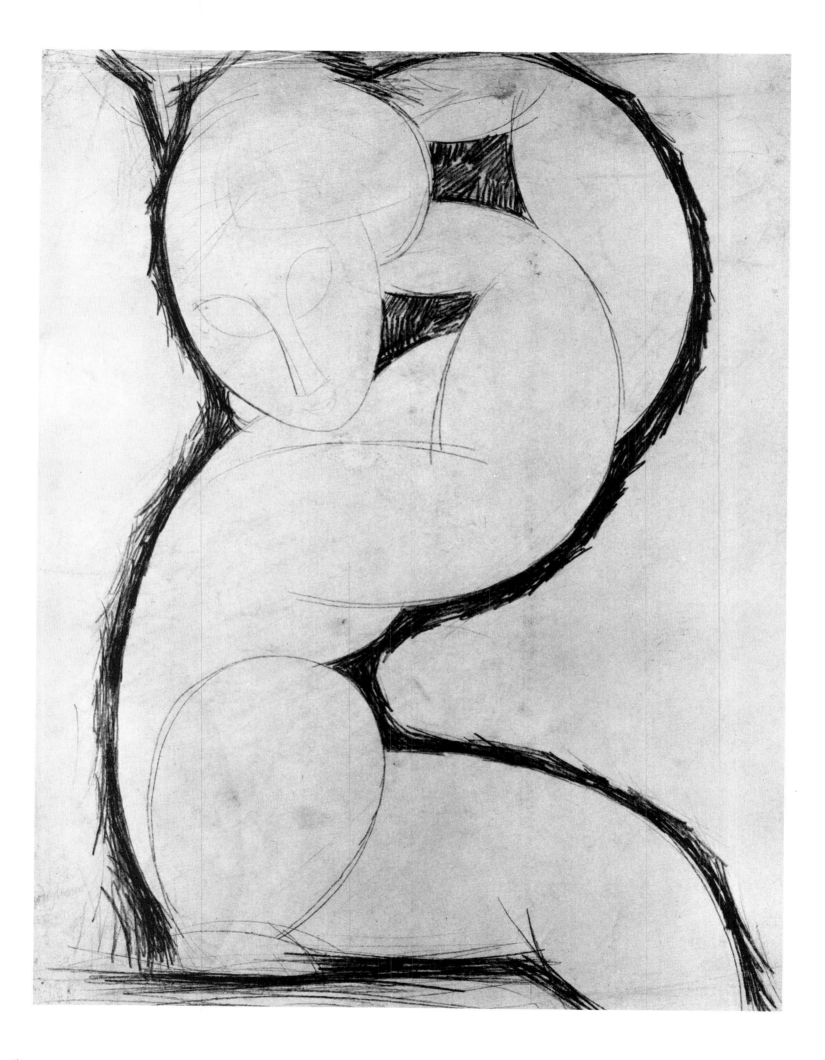

70

72

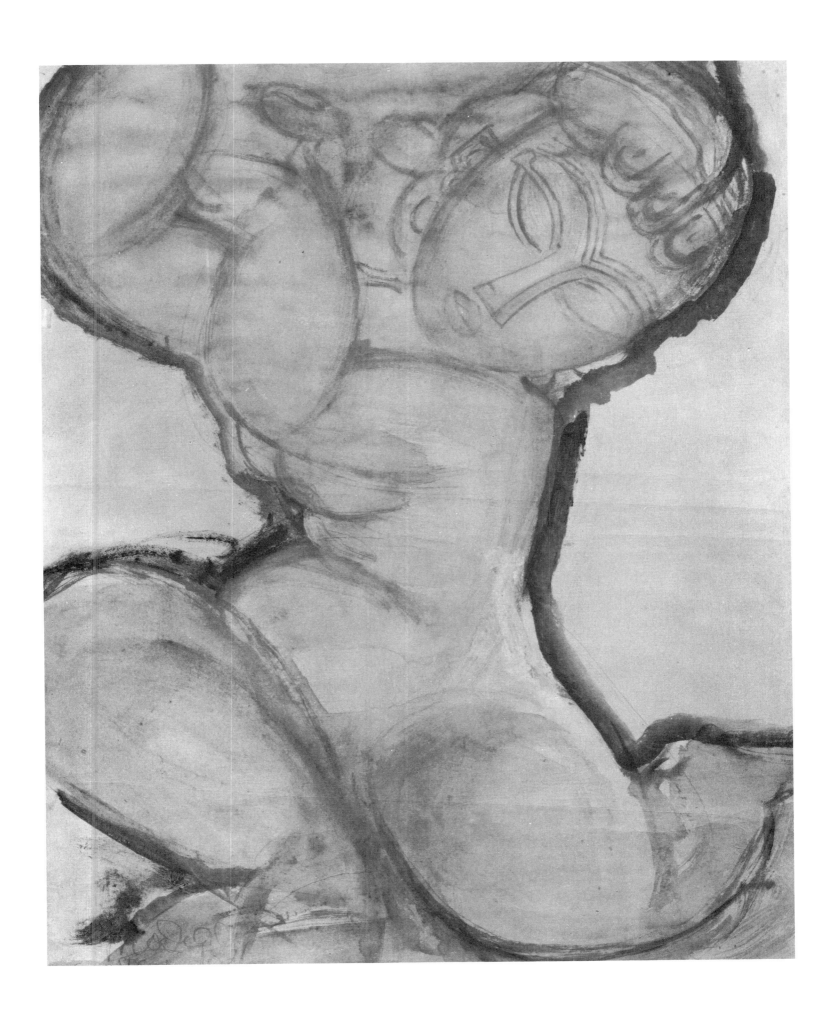

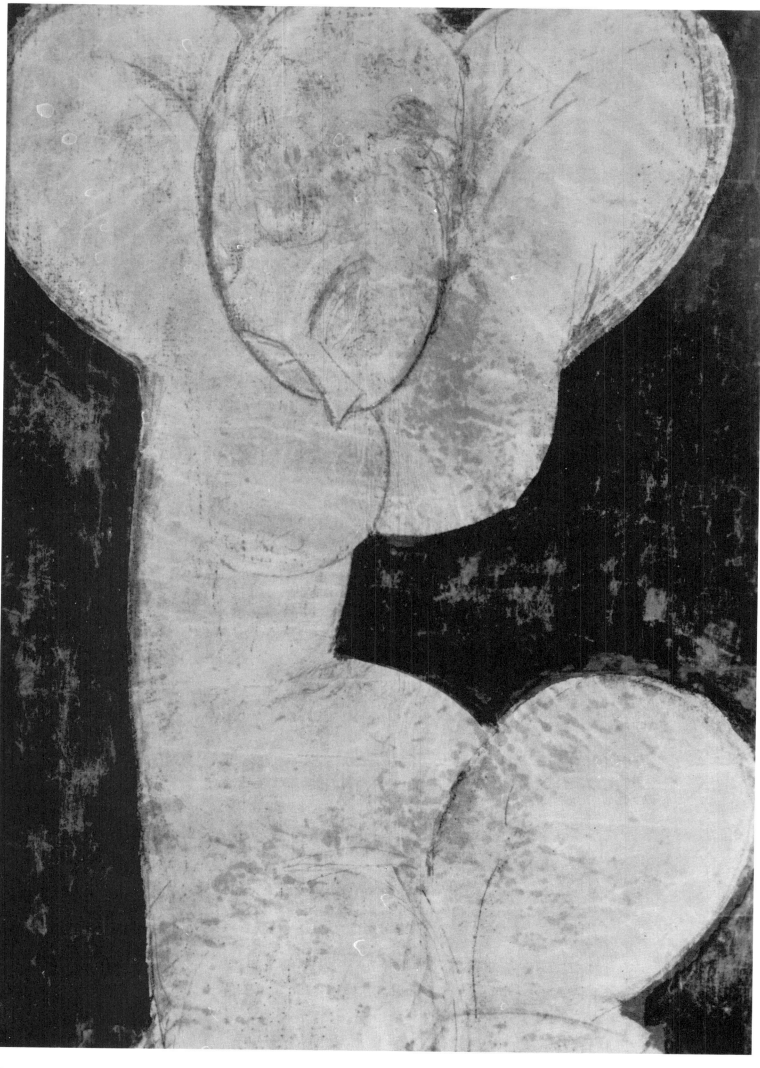

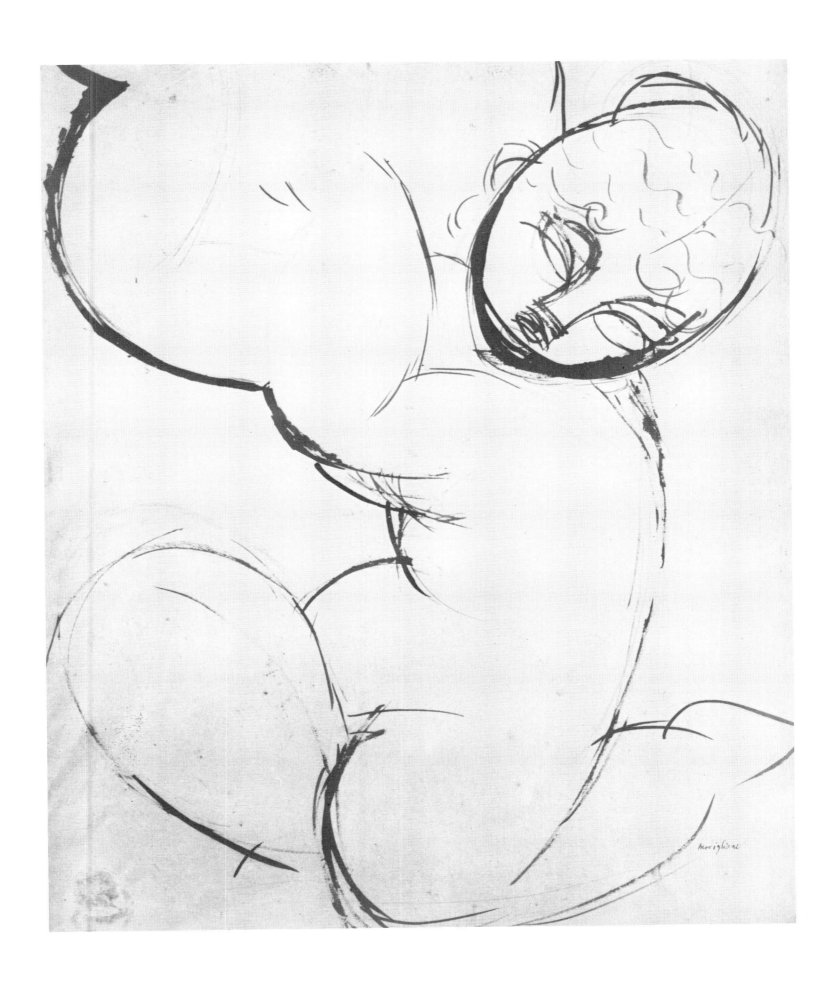

84